I bought a 400 piece Jigsaw of Dublin City, but 6 pieces were missing.
All the way from Christchurch to James Street...

I thought to myself "someone is taking Liberties"

I'm in a support group called 'Dance Addicts Anonymous'

You have to book your spot though. You can't just waltz in off the street!

My 3 worst subjects in school were Maths and History.

...I think....

There's no posters of me in the Sheriff's office..

I know when I'm not wanted

A guy showed up at my fire station and said he had two arm chairs and a settee for us..

I said "I'm sorry. I can't accept suites from strangers"

It makes me very uncomfortable when people ask to borrow my pillows

My wife says she's leaving me 'cos of my obsession with Poker...

She's bluffing!!

(I'll deal with it if it happens)

I'm a big football fan!

(I much rather them to regular size footballs)

I'm watching a great new documentary on Netflix about hotels..

There's four seasons in it

I'm teaching a class of trainee mechanics and I just spent the day explaining combustion of fuels in a petrol engine..

It's exhausting!

I know what acronyms are now. But I didn't initially.

A lot of actors have devoted fans, but Bruce Willis has the most Die Hard ones

There's a big problem at the moment with people getting addicted to Motown music.

If anyone here is affected...reach out! I'll be there!

The problem with being addicted to Motown music is you think you're over it, but the temptations are always there!

The key is to stop listening to Motown music for at least three weeks...four Tops!

I managed to get my wife into my archery club...

I had to pull a few strings.

When Brigette Neilson divorced Sylvester Stallone...

did she tell people she just got out of a Rocky marriage?

My friend had asked me to be his 'best man' and now he tells me I'm demoted to 'groomsman'...

I'm speechless!!

I keep getting grief off people in work!

I hate being an undertaker..

My dentist is away on holidays...

But she has someone filling in for her.

The part of my body I love the most is my Aorta..

From the bottom of my heart!

My nephew has just started work as a chiropodist...

It's early days though, he's still finding his feet...

I got arrested for poaching!

But the judge said "how you cook your eggs is your own business!"

"Omletting you off"

I have a phobia for 'Recliner Chairs'

I have it since...umm...going way back....

It's actually a deep seated fear!

And it's become very common. People need to sit up and take notice!

There's a support group for people who suffer with it. I've been a long standing member

We even have a committee made up of a Secretary, Treasurer and PRO.

When I heard it was being filmed in Ireland, I tried my best to get a part in 'Braveheart'

I even rang up Mel Gibson, but he put me on HOLD! HOLD! HOLD!

They got rid of the windows in my gym...

No pane no gain!

In the last census, it turns out 5% of Irish households have their own water supply...

It's well for some!

And now I will reveal my favourite prolonged sound from a percussion instrument...

Drum roll....

I spilled water on my C.V. and I had it hanging out the back to dry...

And my wife was laughing at me... I said to her "my career is on the line here!"

I think I have invented a guitar with strings that never move...

Stay tuned...

Imagine not knowing how to play Monopoly?!

What are the chances?!

My top 20 things to change about my life now that I've turned 50:

1. More exercise
2. Eat healthier
3. Think about lists first, before assigning large numbers to them...

I just saw a great movie called 'The 20 foot fishing rod'

What a cast!

There was some great lines in it.

It left me reeling!

We're only one compass reading away from winning this orienteering competition...

But we're not outta the woods yet!

I just completed my carpentry exam...

Nailed it!

Good job I had my hammer or I'd be screwed!

I asked my local pharmacist if they sold insoles for sneakers?

She said 'No. Have you tried boots?"

I said "yeah, but my feet sweat in all footwear"

In an effort to get more sleep, myself and my wife bought a memory foam mattress...

But instead, we stayed up all night talking about the good old days.

Does everyone think of the same thing when someone mentions 'The Scouts'?

I think knot.

Last night I was supposed to go to a lecture about the mating rituals of prehistoric man..

But it was knocked on the head.

I met John Piper in town and asked him how his brother Peter was?

He said "hard to say really…"

I'm a big movie fan!

I think it was Tom Hank's best film!

My local shop stocks my favourite fabric softener...

It's a great source of comfort to me.

My wife always sends me to the shop and the other day I came back and told her "they had no 'Mars Bars'. But I did get you a 'Milky Way'? if that's any constellation?

She told me the other day to "get mayonnaise, but to make sure to get regular mayonnaise! Not the Light stuff! you got the Light stuff the last time!"
Anyway, I got the regular mayonnaise, but it turns out I had the wrong brand.
F##king hellman!!

My local barber is now serving dinners as well as haircuts...

I had the steak with all the trimmings.

I asked my friend "do you mind if I run something by you?"

He said to me "you're not really getting the hang of this relay race are you?"

I've come up with an eco-friendly way of making more room in cow sheds..

My design involves putting in another floor just under the roof...

I think my 'Cattle Attic Converter' is gonna make me a fortune!!

I was looking for a new 'welcome mat' and it turns out that a shop in my village sells them...

Right on my doorstep!

So I turned up to audition for the Elvis musical and I said "Hi everyone!
It's really great to be here! I'm so excited! Thanks so much for having me! Is there any particular song you want me to sing?"

The director said "A little less conversation would be great"

I said "Alright. I was only trying to be friendly"

Someone just put a note under my door with the word 'single' written on it....

That can mean only one thing.

I told my friend that my uncle was a song writer back in the 80s and he wrote Paula Abdul's biggest hit...

He said "Straight up?" I said "Yeah! Why would I lie about that?'

We've been racking our brains trying to come up with new ways to test the airbags on our cars..

But we keep hitting a brick wall.

Myself and the wife are in an S+M club.

It's full up though. They're not accepting any new members. Our hands are tied.

So there's no point in SUBMITTING an application form.

Personally, I'd like to give everyone a fair crack of the whip..

But they won't allow it. Why? Beats me!

Detectives only go on holidays when the case is closed.

My wife joined a skydivers club a few months back and she's
already won the
'Best newcomer award'

She landed on her feet I tell ya!

They had to cancel this weeks meeting as too many members were
sick. They must have come down with something.

I don't like shortcuts. I go out of my way to avoid them.

I just bought another 'Kinder egg' with nothing in the middle of it...

I'm not surprised anymore.

They reckon now that drinking tequila can help fight COVID.

I'd take that with a pinch of salt!

(although, it might be worth a shot?)

"Holmes? How did you know the killer used that red, Gravelly rock as the murder weapon?"

"Sedimentary my dear Watson! Sedimentary"

I asked my friend if he'd like to come to my house for a curry on Saturday..

He said "Tai?"

I said " not at all! Just dress casual"

The wardrobe lady at my line dancing class is very strict!

She Always keeps me in check

I called into the Butcher and I asked him if he had any books on understanding professions?

He sent me to the library. Turns out my neighbour works there, but she keeps it quite...

I asked her if she had the new book on how to understand jokes?

She said "probably won't get it 'til next week" and I said "yeah. that's the one"

I noticed a poster on the wall for a comedy show, to be held in the library and I thought to myself 'that's a novel idea'

But then I wondered why they didn't book me? I was like "Fine!"

I'm not gonna read into it too much..

I know loads of Italian words. Like 'bruschetta'...and that's just for starters!

At cooking class the other night, I baked a pyramid shaped cake...

That'll be hard to top!

As my late uncle Tom used to say...

"sorry to keep you waiting"

The saleswoman laughed at me when I asked If I could keep the hanger...

That's the last time I buy a 737 off her airline company!

Every year I buy the same brand of sun cream and I don't know why?

I think the number on the front could be a factor?

I'm performing as Tina Turner at our local 'Stars in their eyes' competition this weekend, but I've decided I'm gonna sing 'Proud Mary'...

As I'm not feeling the best

When I was a kid, I'd rub my feet on the carpet and give my sisters a static shock...

But when my parents found out, they grounded me.

I uses to work on the door of a department store, telling customers they looked great...

I was an Insecurity guard.

I'm always amazed at how many French words are in the English language…

I was only saying it to my chauffer when we were enroute to a rendezvous with my fiancé at a buffet in a café in a Cul De sac….but we couldn't think of any….

I saw online that there's a town in France called 'Guillotine' and I think I might head off there for a weekend….or that neck of the woods.

I keep having a recurring dream where I think I'm a horse...

Last 5 nights on the trot!!

My uncle retired from his job making biscuits for Cadburys...

He hasn't lifted a finger since...

I've had to close down my organ transport business...

It's with a heavy heart that I'm doing my last delivery today.

I got fired from my job at the forestry for paying the lumberjacks half the going rate..

I Can't believe they fell for that!!

(It was the branch manager that twigged it! He kept a log book)

I was once in a band called 'Small Font'

We never got to headline a gig.

The new urinals we got fitted in our station are faulty...

Luckily, the suppliers said they'd stand over them.

That's the last time I buy a cheap sat nav online...

I'm not going down that road again!

My wife was deleting apps from her phone and accidently deleted her Fitbit app...

She lost the run of herself!

I was getting on a plane and the guy in front of me had no bag...

he had a crate Of blue, long neck bottles....

and I thought to myself "that's wicked carry on!"

I did a comedy gig for air traffic controllers one night and my jokes
went straight over their heads...

but then I told the a Covid joke and they all got it!

Myself and my wife have joined a nudist club...

We'd nothing on one weekend, so we decided to try it....

It's great for our relationship because no one wears the trousers...

But I'm not happy with how the club is being run lately, so I'm gonna call
down to the chairman this Saturday and have it out with him.

I was in an electrical shop yesterday and they had a brand of kettle
called 'Marsh'

I was in my element!!

When I was a kid I used to eat caterpillars...

I still get butterflies in my stomach just thinking about it!

I had an appointment with my tailor and he never showed up?!
I nearly had a fit!

I told him I don't need him anyway and
He said "Alright! Suit yourself!"

I can never understand people who like to use 'idioms'?

Each to their own I suppose.

I call my wife 'The Archaeologist' 'cos she's always giving me digs..

And she has my life in ruins!

Kurt Russell is to do a remake of his famous horror movie in Helsinki...

I can't wait to see the Finnish thing.

When I was growing up, my parents never believed in having favourites..

It's the main reason our Bookie shop closed down.

(someone tried to buy it recently and I told them it's been closed for years. They said 'that makes no odds" and I said " I know! It's been closed for years!")

Ironically, the song 'Cocaine' by Eric Clapton is mostly guitar solos and
only has a few lines in it.

My wife is leaving me because of my obsession with car parts…

It brakes my heart..

I'm so choked up about it..

People told me the day we got hitched, that it wouldn't last!

And I wouldn't mind, but I used to spoiler!!

I'm just gonna have to move on and wiper from my memories.

I won a rodeo competition and they gave me a nice watch for first prize...

I thought it was worth a few bucks...

But it turns out it was a knock off!

I'm haunted by the time I set up my camera tripod up the wrong way...

I still get flashbacks

I joined the 'Procrastinators society of Ireland' last year and they still haven't sent me

my membership card!

(I hope I don't need it to get into the Christmas party this June)

My friend is an auctioneer who only sells terraced houses...

He's semi retired.

I just witnessed A truck carrying strawberries overturn on the Naas Road!

I had to jam on the brakes!

(the Police have closed of a lane to preserve the scene)

I'm part of a synchronised surfing team..

We have a chat before we get into the water, to make sure we're all on the same wave

I still haven't paid my membership fees for my pottery class…

There'll be kilns!

My wife says she doesn't like my mirrored sunglasses..

But that's no reflection on me

The army barracks in the Curragh is nice...

But the drill yard is always the centre of attention.

I was heading down there yesterday, but I had to take a detour 'cos of Major road works..

So I drove in that General direction but ended up on Private property.

My wife says that she's gonna leave me 'cos of my obsession with 'Status Quo'

I said "Whatever you want!"

We had a competition once in school to see who could write a 3 page essay the fastest…

I won by huge margin.

I got a new job working as a glazer and I'm shattered!

Plus the guys I'm working with are no crack.

It's a pane in the hole to be honest.

I was up in the attic and I found all my 'Dylan', 'Marley' and 'Segar' CDs..

I'd say they're worth a few Bob now.

I got sacked from my job at the morgue for filling human organs with Helium..

I just thought it was a bit of light hearted fun!

We formulate a plan before every choir practice...

Just So we are all singing off the same hymn sheet.

I got arrested for robbing a haybarn but I got out on bail.

I recon someone grassed me up!

I ran the Berlin marathon years ago...

Half way around I hit a wall.

I heard that Dublin Bus are to get new electric buses...

I wonder will they have a conductor?

And will they get rid of the current fleet?

Or will they charge more to bring you Ohm?

There's a 'Mr.Vain' competition in my local pub tonight...

I fancy myself to win it.

I wasn't able to provide a stool sample for a medical in work today, but my friend Steve gave me one of his..

Thanks Steve! You did me a solid!

I've finally convinced my local show shop to stock up to size 14 from now on...

It was no small feet I tell you!

I love reading books and articles about Nostradamus.

I go through them like there's no tomorrow.

There's a condition where people constantly put metals into conversations..

And I'm lead to believe it runs in my family.

There's an big write up on 'merging traffic' in today's newspaper..

It's a pull-out section.

I was DJing at a wedding last week and just after I put on 'Baggy Trousers', a big fight broke out!

I thought to myself "we need to stop this madness!" or someone could be Ska'd for life!

My postman is gone on holidays...

He got a great deal on a package holiday. I hear it's an all Mail resort.

When it comes to people who wear Black
and white in work...

I think referees are second to nun!

When i worked as a referee, i exposed a
lot of wrongdoing in the organisation and
i was commended as a whistle-blower

And when i retired, they gave me a great send off

I'm thinking of taking up a belly dancing class at my local community centre, but I'm not sure if I can get an hour off every Tuesday evening…

I might have to Jiggle things around a bit.

My friend was supposed to call around and help me put up a clothes line, but he never showed up…

He's left me high and dry.

Making omelettes in space…

It's not all it's cracked up to be.

When I was a ventriloquist, all my puppets were made of lego…

I'd wake up every morning and think to myself "I need to get my act together!"

I met a guy in the pub last night who told me he how much he loved Roger Moore and I told him how much I loved Pierce Brosnan...

We Bonded over a few pints..

I signed my 6 year old up for an after school cocktail making class...

"Cos he's not great at mixing..

I'm gonna film myself, the next time I go fishing....

Hopefully I can stream it online...

Maybe Netflix might be interested....

I woke up and thought to myself that it's a lovely Crisp morning...

So I ate a bag of Taytos and half a box of Pringles.

My dad was always very old fashioned, and he believed it was his job to
bring home the bacon..

Which left Denny's with no choice but to sack him as their delivery driver.

He went rasher! When he got the chop.

And they didn't give him any redundancy either... not a sausage!

One of Irelands biggest landowners has passed away and left all his land to a bunch of charities...

I think there's grounds for Concern!

My favourite word in the English language is one that people don't like to hear..

It starts with a 'C' and it rhymes with a type of old Irish currency....

I just love when people get their 'Cumupence'

I'm wreaked! I have a new job cleaning the E-Flow cameras on the M50...

It takes its toll on you!

I rang up Tallaght hospital to see how my friend was doing and the Nurse told me that he "was gone to a better place"

I was shocked!! Until she then gave me the phone number of the Blackrock Clinic..

My friend Joe has spent the last few days plastering the front of Clerys...

He's been working round the clock!

I heard you won a female sheep on the Farmers journal.

Gimme Ewe!

I told the wife I just bought a block of Mitchelstown cheese and she said "There's no cheese grater!?"

I said "I know! It really is the best cheese!"

It was so hot this summer, I would get to the beach early to beat the crowds…

But then the Gardai took my hurley off me and arrested me for assault.

I'm delighted that An Post have asked me to design a new envelope...

I'm looking forward to putting my stamp on it!

Some people are saying i shouldn't have gotten the job and that its mail privilege...

And I'm glad that was addressed!

If I hear any more on the matter...I'll keep you posted...

(That joke always gets a laugh if the delivery is good)

When I was single in my mid-thirties, my friends were forever trying to set me up...

They'd ring the Gardai and tell them I committed loads of crimes!

I love printing missing livestock posters...

 I could do it til...

Last weekend I was supposed to go Donegal on a creative writing course...

But I couldn't make it up.

I saw an advert on TV that said 'if you drive a tractor, you must hold a licence'

Those things are hard enough to steer with 2 hands!?

I told my wife that she couldn't join my photography club and she snapped!

She said I was trying to shutter out! And that I was so negative!

Remember the night you drank all the Rum based cocktails?

Mai tai remind you?!

My nephew works on the sites. He got a job in Specsavers.

Actually I got it for him! I've loads of contacts.

My doctor told me I'm off milk and cheese..

How dairy!!

I remember when i first met Bono. It was at
a fancy dress party and i had 3 big propellers
around head and a pull cord hanging from my chin...

i walked up to him and said "Bono! I'm a big fan!"

Later that night it all turned sour though...
We were playing 'Twister' and he kept trying to
knock us off balance...
He pushed me over the Edge that night!!

I'm trying to get his duet with Mary J Blige voted
as the best duet of all time. If you vote for it I'll give
you a €10 voucher that can be used in any shop..

Remember, All for One and One for all!

I'm in a new advert for 'Subway'...

I've a small role..

And I'm the main character!

They're now selling the George Forman grill at 'Spar!'

It's half price too. A knockout deal!

I just filmed a movie in Wexford. It had loads of violence and bloodshed!

It was beyond Gorey!

If ever I'm having a stressful day , I like to put on a beanie hat, pick up a guitar and tell people I'm in U2..

Just to take the Edge off

They were gonna build a second Newgrange..

But then Covid hit and it never saw the light of day.

It was reported that kids in my local school have decide to boycott the catholic church and a spokesperson for the school has said there has been no confirmation yet…

Must be true so?

I get sexually aroused by sunrises..

It wasn't until I started working nights that it first came to light.

They are making a documentary about Covid hitting a small seaside town in Wicklow..

It's called the 'Great Brittas Bay cough'

My favourite magazine is 'Chiropractor monthly '

i have all the back issues.

I keep them on disc.

Up in my Si Attic.

They have some cracking articles in them

My friend asked me if he could come onto my podcast…

I said "Be my guest"

I'm a Eucharistic minister at my local church, so everyone calls me 'Mr.Eucharist'

It's my Alter ego

A container carrying 'Fairy Liquid' bottles fell off a ship in Rosslare this morning…

Locals say they have been washing up on the beach all day…

Police were on the scene earlier, but the coast is clear now.

I find the people in Tenerife swear a lot, so I always go to Lanzarote..

'Cos I never resort to bad language!

My first job was working as a Roadie...

A friend of mine was a Roadie, so I thought I'd be One Too....One Too...

My friend Peg finished her fashion degree last month…

She's already got her own clothes line!

A woman on the street last night started shouting at me saying "your hair is like a poodles fur! You have ears like a chihuahua !! You walk like a dachshund!!

I've no idea why she was giving me dogs abuse?

Our local Ice cream man is retiring, so we had a whip around for him.

It's about time! He's 99! (or soda say)

We often respond to fire alarms at big shopping outlets.

The other day we went to Ikea and everyone was confused 'cos they had been told to go to the 'Assembly Area'

The week before we went to B&Q and everyone was at different areas around the car park...

I asked the manager "Do you do fire drills?" and he said "No. We do Bosch and DeWalt"

When I worked at 'Pixar', I fell out with a colleague over how to draw 'Walle'

It was a year later that we made up

Auctioneers don't drink coffee

They like proper tea

I got a huge painting of an elephant for my sitting room..

Nobody ever comments on it?!

A bank where your savings doesn't grow??

Not interested!

My wife says I argue too much..

That's bullshit!

I'm gonna try beat the world record for the longest time spent on a swing

I really need to push myself!

A monk died at our local monastery and out of respect, they had a minutes talking.

Are maths teachers overweight because of all the take aways?

*We responded to a crash on the M50 involving a
foot locker van...*

A guy called Clark was the sole occupant...

*Witnesses say he had the boot down and was
 giving it welly when he crashed...
but he says that's a croc!*

traffic was clogged up for miles...

*His solicitor showed up and told him to thread
carefully and not converse with anyone!
he said "let me sandal this"*

*Anyway, we brought him to hospital and
Dr.Martin said "heel be fine"*

It was at exactly 77 minutes past 7 this morning that I realised..

That new alarm clock I got off Wish.com was crap!

We had a great time in the pub last night slagging off Formula 1 drivers
From the 90s.

We started slagging Senna, Hakkinen and Mansell...
After that, it was down Hill all the way!

My friend gave me a tip to buy 'Bulmers' stock...

But I got done for in cider trading.

I know I slagged off 'Preparation H' before..

For the record, on the whole I think it's great!

I'm writing a song about digging for coal...

In A minor

I disliked the last Tom Cruise movie so much, I turned it off after 20 minutes..

I ended up losing my job as a projectionist at the 'Odean Cinema' in Tallaght over it!

I said before that Bela Lugosi was the first actor to play Dracula, but he wasn't.
And I also said that Keanu Reeves played Dracula, but he actually played his barrister.

So I was wrong on both counts!

Never pay plumbers by the hour!

They'll drain you finances and they won't do a tap!

I decide i love sandwiches so much...

I'm gonna start a club!

Anyone can join after filling out the forms…
And once its full, people can wait for the next batch..

It'll be a great way to meat people..

we'll have a roll call..

lettuce put our heads together and come up with a
good name for it…ciabatta be a good one!

I told my GP to write himself a prescription for some nice tablets…

"Go on. Treat yourself!"

When I worked in the 'Guinness' fire brigade, we would put out fires with water..

Then wait a minute and top it off with foam.

I have a lot of issues with the Fire Brigade..

But my problems with the guy running it is my chief complaint.

I used to service the ladders in the fire brigade, but I recently quit…

I rung up the Chief and when I was put through to his extension..
I said "I'll level with you. I have to step down"

He said "Thanks a for all the hard work! You're a ledge!"

I spelled 'eczema' wrong on a form yesterday and the nurse gave out to me.

I thought to myself "that's a little rash"

(I put that 'eczema' joke up on social media and it got a huge reaction!)

My uncle works in the council and he got promoted from 'roads' to 'footpaths'

It's a step up for him. He's career is on the right path.

I'm gonna go out on a limb here and say that firefighters shouldn't have to
rescue cats from trees

When I worked in the airport police, people would get annoyed when I would
check their boarding cards getting off the plane...

And I could see where they were coming from.

We responded to an Ice cream van on fire on the M50...

When we got there, we put out cones...

Hundreds and thousands of cars were stuck in traffic! it created a ripple effect! Loads of sundae drivers!

There were reporters on the scene trying to get the scoop

And the driver was only back to work after getting covid.. He was a wafer two weeks.... just flaked out on the couch

And to top it off, the van had a sprinkle system, but it failed!

"My wife booked a weekend for us in some posh manor in Limerick"

"Adare?"

"no. it was all her idea"

I competed in the 'world interfering games'

I won a Meddle! And a Hamper!

The guys at work are always slipping 'Viagra' into my tea..

I think they're trying to get it up for me!

I rang up a car insurance company and asked them if they could give me a quote?

The guy said "ask not what your country can do for you, but what you
can do for your country"

I told my 'Bermuda triangle' joke at a gig last night...

Lost the whole crowd! There's no coming back after that..

So far its only me that has renewed my membership to the Chesney Hawkes fanclub...

I've joined weight watchers...

I'm doing night security at a gym.

I got kicked out of my conspiracy theories club...

I couldn't believe it!

"i like to wear headphones when i play snooker, so i can listen to some
gentle ballads"

"Acoustic?"

"Oh yeah! you need one of those too!"

I've been down to goffs a few times to watch the snooker, but i always
get stuck in traffic and end up arriving late...

i can't catch a break!

I had to get circumcised and I asked the Doctor "will everything…
..be….um….

He said "Everything will be just fine down there!
… sorry for cutting you short"

(He did a great job. I left him a tip)

My mate is always saying "this f**king water! The water tastes F**king
Terrible!"

He has no filter…

So I first cheated on my wife in July 2012. Then in April 2013 and again
In September 2013…

(Sorry, I'm just trying to get my affairs in order)

I've hoping my new acupuncturist can pin point what's wrong with me..

The last fella I had was useless prick!

On my first day back to the sperm bank after lockdown, the staff gave
me a great welcome...

One of them shouted "get a load of this guy!"

(During lockdown we had to send samples by post and make sure to
 register the package in case of any come back)

Dublin is to host the world Dominos championship...

It's lined up for early November...

I think there's still spots available.

I don't want people finding out I get sexually aroused my tomato sauce...

I'm afraid my wife will spill the beans on me.

Kevin Costner gets sexually aroused by Lego!

If you build it...

My wife says she's leaving me because of my addiction
to quiz shows...

I'm worried my marriage is in Jeopardy!

I've pushed he to her tipping point!!

I think it would be pointless to chase her to make her
mind
up now...if i play my cards right, she might change her
mind...

Although the odds on that are about 15 to 1.... i fear its
the countdown to the end of my marriage ...if the price
is
right, i might get to keep the house

I was hanging around the Curragh and a bunch of Jockeys asked me to join them in
a football game…

It seems they were short men…

I left my job at the 'Tipp ex' factory after I exposed a big cover up.

Everyone blanked me after that.

After lockdown, my wife was so excited to be going back to the hairdressers,
that she filmed it on her phone…

I edited it, so it was just the highlights.

I wanted to go out to the air show and I asked a taxi driver "whats the fair to Bray?"

He said "I think they're the bones in your back?"

I just got a part in a new TV show. Every week we're gonna murder someone
In uniform...

We just shot a pilot.

I also got a part in a remake of 'The Great Train robbery', but I still haven't gotten the script...

I don't know what the hold-up is?!

I met my wife at the world 'Tetris' championships...

I brought her out onto the dance floor and threw a few shapes..
After that, everything just fell into place.

During lockdown I took place in an online farting competition...

I logged out by mistake.

I was late for ship building class...

my instructor gave me a stern talking to.

he said "you can't just cruise in here at whatever time suits you!"

I was wreaked from the night before..i thought i was gonna keel over

*I didn't mind him giving out to me but I'd pre Ferry didn't do it in front
of my work colleagues. He's lucky i didn't deck him!*

*(that's a lot of ship puns! i may have gone overboard?
 or hopefully you're in knots laughing?)*

They've changed the chef at our local golf club...

A little birdie tells me the food isn't up to par with the last chef.

The club is 5 miles from my house,
so it's a fairway to go for your tee..

And i heard he had a club sandwedge as one of the main
courses? and it tastes bogey!

We normally pop in after a 4 ball. I'm not one to complain,
but i know the other three wood!

It was me that screwed up the sandwich order!

I'll take the wrap.

There's a medical condition where people put the names of countries into conversations…

I'm Ghana say there's Norway that will ever happen me!

My wife isn't talking to me , so I bought her an electric fan…

I thought it might clear the air…

Hopefully it'll all blow over soon…

My wife broke my new iPhone, so I'm in the process of getting another one..

I'm on Tinder, plenty of fish, Bumble…

My wife loves the band '4 Non Blondes' but I could never get into them...

And I try! Oh my god do I try!

There's a new boxing craze. It's the same as boxing, but you can't defend yourself...

You get hooked very easily!

My neighbour told me that a good way to get a baby to sleep is to bring it for a
drive...

but to be honest, the sound off the motorbike and the wind in his face, just
made him even more awake!?

I got kicked out of the pessimist's society of Ireland...

I bloody knew that was gonna happen!!

(they never liked me because I used to put out too many chairs before the meetings. I'm thinking of starting up my own pessimist society, but I don't think it will be as good)

My doctor told me that my balance was off and I'm inclined to agree with him...

But then my wife told me it wasn't and I believed her. (I'm easily swayed)

I don't like elevators.

I take lots of steps to avoid them.

I wanted to learn how to play golf, so I went on a Course...

I'm not a fan of festivals. I think there are 2 types of people in the world:
Those who can manoeuvre around tents with ease and those who can't.

And I know which camp I fall into!

Printed by Amazon Italia Logistica S.r.l.
Torrazza Piemonte (TO), Italy

41243536R00047